MW00901650

Own Your Future

Kristen Judd

Copyright © 2017 Kristen Judd

All rights reserved.

ISBN-10: 1974643727
ISBN-13: 978-1974643721
Library of Congress Control Number: 2017913864

DEDICATION

To my three kids, Daelynn, Gunnar and Brody, who have supported me over the last few years. This is my opportunity to give back to you and give you the gift of owning your success and future! You are capable of big things and the only person who is holding you back is you!

To my husband, who has supported me and helped me get to the space where I am at now. You are my rock! Thank you!

Fellow Goal Achiever-

I hope you spend a little time reading this first. Maybe you are little like me and you have seen success in the past, but you didn't have any science to it. It felt like it just happened. In my early year's I found success in high school and college both academically and in athletics. Then things just sort of changed. In 2001, I was forced into entrepreneurship. Man, it was harder than I thought! Everyone said to 'write down your goals' and to be S.M.A.R.T about it. I did exactly as I was told and it just didn't seem to work. Learning to effectively write down my goals was a journey, I had to learn how to do this and I had to be very intentional about it. I had to learn how the mind works and how the mind works for you.

Over the years I have explored and tried several different success techniques. I've tried writing my goals on individual printed goal sheets, working with accountability partners, master mind groups, leads groups, you name ... and I bet I tried. I found bits and pieces that I liked in everything I tried but I found journaling was the one thing really held me accountable. My problem was that I just could not find a journal that pulled all the pieces together and over the years I have tried A LOT of journals. My goal was to draw from my experiences and build a tool, a journal, which would guide me and keep me focused on my journey to success.

As I mentioned earlier, I had to understand how the mind works and once I did, everything came into play! The mind needs direction and consistency; you need to literally be telling your mind what to do every day. I have found that there is no better way to keep your mind focused than through the daily use of a journal. Once I started doing this it became so much easier to achieve my goals and I became addicted to it ... it became a habit. Everything we do in life is about habits and if you develop the habit of focused journaling, you will find success. Habits are the #1 determining factor to whether you will be successful or not.

This journal is designed to be used, not just every day, but all day; morning, noon and night and even those gaps in between. It is meant to keep you on track toward your goals with clear focus on those actions and activities that will continuously work to move you forward. As an added bonus, I have even included some micro meditation and positive influence for you each day. A good business plan is developed on 90 day increments and I have built that same model into this journal.

In the details to follow and in the pages of the journal itself, you will find the exact actions that I realized changed my business and my success … in following my journal and my plan I have literally transformed my life. It is my sincere hope that you find the same success I have in using this journal. Make it a habit, maybe even get a little addicted to it, and sit back and watch your focused efforts compound.

The Journaling Process

Meditation: Start every day with 5 deeps breaths. This is just a small meditation technique to keep your mind calm, ready and focused. I have found that meditation can be extremely powerful and wanted to be sure that it was part of my daily routine. You can do a guided meditation if you would like but at least take those five deep breaths.

Write Down Your Goal Everyday: You may have noticed that I said Goal – not Goals, this is not something to be overlooked. Your mind is powerful, but it honestly was not built for multitasking! This really Powerful thing happens when you write down your Goal – your focus becomes laser sharp and your brain starts to go to work for you. When you continuously put that goal out there, on paper, your brain feels the desire to find ways to make that goal become a reality. Oh, that guilt you feel when you are not on task – that is your brain telling you "Hey, we are getting off track".

Why Your Goal is Important: Why do you want this goal? Why would achieving this goal change everything for you? What would it do for you? I found it to be really important to be connected and passionate about my goal.

Gratitude: Physically writing down your Gratitudes every day is Essential. Doing this puts your body and mind in the right vibration to be able to attract more of the same and even have everything around conspire to do the same. If you have not been doing this, it is a muscle that takes practice to develop, but I promise it gets easier and easier the more you do it.

All In Massive Action: These are the things that you really need to get done on a daily basis to propel you forward toward your goal. We all know that life happens every day and the list of tasks and responsibilities can be daunting at times, but always make time to do the things that move you closer to your goal. The most important things first.

Ideas: Remember I said this journal is designed to be used, not just every day, but all day; morning, noon and night and even those gaps in between. Well, ideas fall in the 'gaps in between'. I often have those moments where an idea will come up out of nowhere – generally, for me; it has something to do with marketing. When that idea pops into your head, write it down and keep a record of it.

Areas for Improvement: This is to be done at the end of the day; it's your time to reflect. Write down what you learned and what areas may need some work. Be clear about what you need to focus on to make better.

I'm Grateful Tonight For: Always end the day by writing down what went right. Your brain will tend to focus on the last thing it sees before you shut down for the night – give it something positive to feed on all night!

Every week actions. These are every week actions or activities that can really enhance your life and/or your business. It can range from birthday calls, networking, business calls, working out, personal development, etc. For example, you will say the activity is to work out and the goal is to work out 3 times a week. Each day of the week you will chart your results. You will mark the days that you worked out, add them up under achieved and subtract them from the goal to get your net result. Did you keep your promise to yourself? CONSISTENCY is the goal. Consistency compounded over time is what makes the biggest difference in everything that we do. We all know what we need to do to get the goal... now just go do it!

Your habits will predict your future. Make sure you are practicing the habits.

I, _____ commit to working
and achieving this goal:

_____

_____

_____

_____

over the next 90 days.

Once I reach this goal, I will reward myself with

_____

_____

_____

X_____

Now, let's get started!

Monday

Take 5 deep breaths

> *"Financial Freedom is available to those that learn about it and work for it." - Robert Kiyosaki*

The goal written in present tense:

_____

_____

Why is this goal important:

_____

_____

_____

I'm so grateful for:

➤ _____

➤ _____

➤ _____

➤ _____

➤ _____

All In Massive Action Items

1. _____

2. _____

3. _____

4. _____

5. _____

Ideas:

_____

_____

_____

_____

Areas of Improvement:

_____

_____

_____

I'm grateful tonight for:

_____

_____

_____

_____

Every week actions:

Behavior/Action	Goal	M	T	W	TH	F	Sa	Su	Achieved	Net

Tuesday

Take 5 deep breaths

> *"Self-Improvement is the name of the game, and our primary objective is to strengthen yourself, not to destroy an opponent." – Maxwell Maltz*

The goal written in present tense:

_____

_____

Why is this goal important:

_____

_____

_____

I'm so grateful for:

➤ _____

_____

➤ _____

_____

➤ _____

_____

➤ _____

_____

➤ _____

_____

All In Massive Action Items

1. _____

_____

2. _____

_____

3. _____

_____

4. _____

_____

5. _____

_____

Ideas:

_____

_____

_____

_____

Areas of Improvement:

_____

_____

_____

I'm grateful tonight for:

_____

_____

_____

_____

Wednesday

Take 5 deep breaths

> *"Success consists of going from failure to failure without loss of enthusiasm." – Winston Churchill*

The goal written in present tense:

_____

_____

Why is this goal important:

_____

_____

_____

I'm so grateful for:

➤ _____

➤ _____

➤ _____

➤ _____

➤ _____

All In Massive Action Items

1. _____

2. _____

3. _____

4. _____

5. _____

Ideas:

_____

_____

_____

_____

Areas of Improvement:

_____

_____

_____

I'm grateful tonight for:

_____

_____

_____

_____

Thursday

Take 5 deep breaths

> *"Many can argue that reality is as it is, but my experience is that the opposite is exactly true. Reality is ours for the making." – Asara Lovejoy*

The goal written in present tense:

_____

_____

Why is this goal important:

_____

_____

_____

I'm so grateful for:

➢ _____

_____

➢ _____

_____

➢ _____

_____

➢ _____

_____

➢ _____

_____

All In Massive Action Items

1. _____

_____

2. _____

_____

3. _____

_____

4. _____

_____

5. _____

_____

Ideas:

_____
_____
_____
_____

Areas of Improvement:

_____
_____
_____

I'm grateful tonight for:

_____
_____
_____
_____

Friday

Take 5 deep breaths

> *"Visualize this thing that you want, see it, feel it, believe in it. Make your mental blue print, and begin to build." – Robert Collier*

The goal written in present tense:

_____

_____

Why is this goal important:

_____

_____

_____

I'm so grateful for:

➢ _____

➢ _____

➢ _____

➢ _____

➢ _____

All In Massive Action Items

1. _____

2. _____

3. _____

4. _____

5. _____

Ideas:

_____

_____

_____

_____

Areas of Improvement:

_____

_____

_____

I'm grateful tonight for:

_____

_____

_____

_____

Saturday

Take 5 deep breaths

> *"The Universe likes SPEED. Don't delay, don't second-guess, don't doubt. When the opportunity or impulse is there... ACT!" – Joe Vitale*

The goal written in present tense:

_____

_____

Why is this goal important:

_____

_____

_____

I'm so grateful for:

➢ _____

➢ _____

➢ _____

➢ _____

➢ _____

All In Massive Action Items

1. _____

2. _____

3. _____

4. _____

5. _____

Ideas:

_____

_____

_____

_____

Areas of Improvement:

_____

_____

_____

I'm grateful tonight for:

_____

_____

_____

_____

Sunday

Take 5 deep breaths

"Believe you can and you're halfway there." – Theodore Roosevelt

The goal written in present tense:

_____

_____

Why is this goal important:

_____

_____

_____

I'm so grateful for:

➢ _____

➢ _____

➢ _____

➢ _____

➢ _____

All In Massive Action Items

1. _____

2. _____

3. _____

4. _____

5. _____

Ideas:

_____
_____
_____
_____

Areas of Improvement:

_____
_____
_____

I'm grateful tonight for:

_____
_____
_____
_____

Monday

Take 5 deep breaths

> *"More gold had been mined from the minds of men than the earth itself." – Napoleon Hill*

The goal written in present tense:

_____

_____

Why is this goal important:

_____

_____

_____

I'm so grateful for:

➢ _____

_____

➢ _____

_____

➢ _____

_____

➢ _____

_____

➢ _____

_____

All In Massive Action Items

1. _____

_____

2. _____

_____

3. _____

_____

4. _____

_____

5. _____

_____

Ideas:

_____

_____

_____

_____

Areas of Improvement:

_____

_____

_____

I'm grateful tonight for:

_____

_____

_____

_____

Every week actions:

Behavior/Action	Goal	M	T	W	TH	F	Sa	Su	Achieved	Net

Tuesday

Take 5 deep breaths

> *"Cherish your vision and your dreams as they are the children of your soul, the blueprints of your ultimate achievements." – Napoleon Hill*

The goal written in present tense:

_____

_____

Why is this goal important:

_____

_____

_____

I'm so grateful for:

➢ _____

_____

➢ _____

_____

➢ _____

_____

➢ _____

_____

➢ _____

_____

All In Massive Action Items

1. _____

_____

2. _____

_____

3. _____

_____

4. _____

_____

5. _____

_____

Ideas:

_____

_____

_____

_____

Areas of Improvement:

_____

_____

_____

I'm grateful tonight for:

_____

_____

_____

_____

Wednesday

Take 5 deep breaths

> *"Imagination is more important than knowledge. For while knowledge defines all we currently know and understand, imagination points to all we might yet discover and create." – Albert Einstein*

The goal written in present tense:

_____

_____

Why is this goal important:

_____

_____

_____

I'm so grateful for:

➤ _____

➤ _____

➤ _____

➤ _____

➤ _____

All In Massive Action Items

1. _____

2. _____

3. _____

4. _____

5. _____

Ideas:

_____

_____

_____

_____

Areas of Improvement:

_____

_____

_____

I'm grateful tonight for:

_____

_____

_____

_____

Thursday

Take 5 deep breaths

> *"If you want to reach a goal, you must 'see the reaching' in your own mind before you actually arrive at your goal." – Zig Ziglar*

The goal written in present tense:

_____

_____

Why is this goal important:

_____

_____

_____

I'm so grateful for:

➤ _____

➤ _____

➤ _____

➤ _____

➤ _____

All In Massive Action Items

1. _____

2. _____

3. _____

4. _____

5. _____

Ideas:

_____

_____

_____

_____

Areas of Improvement:

_____

_____

_____

I'm grateful tonight for:

_____

_____

_____

_____

Friday

Take 5 deep breaths

> *"Formulate and stamp indelibly on your mind a mental picture of yourself succeeding. Hold this picture tenaciously and never permit it to fade. Your mind will seek to develop this picture!" – Dr. Norman Vincent Peale*

The goal written in present tense:

_____

_____

Why is this goal important:

_____

_____

_____

I'm so grateful for:

➢ _____

➢ _____

➢ _____

➢ _____

➢ _____

All In Massive Action Items

1. _____

2. _____

3. _____

4. _____

5. _____
   _____

Ideas:
_____
_____
_____
_____

Areas of Improvement:
_____
_____
_____

I'm grateful tonight for:
_____
_____
_____
_____

Saturday

Take 5 deep breaths

> *"To Succeed in life, you need three things: A wishbone, a backbone and a funny bone." – Reba McEntire*

The goal written in present tense:

_____

_____

Why is this goal important:

_____

_____

_____

I'm so grateful for:

➤ _____

➤ _____

➤ _____

➤ _____

➤ _____

All In Massive Action Items

1. _____

2. _____

3. _____

4. _____

5. _____

Ideas:

_____

_____

_____

_____

Areas of Improvement:

_____

_____

_____

I'm grateful tonight for:

_____

_____

_____

_____

Sunday

Take 5 deep breaths

> *"Doing the best at this moment puts you in the best place for the next moment." – Oprah Winfrey*

The goal written in present tense:

_____

_____

Why is this goal important:

_____

_____

_____

I'm so grateful for:

➤ _____

➤ _____

➤ _____

➤ _____

➤ _____

All In Massive Action Items

1. _____

2. _____

3. _____

4. _____

5. _____

Ideas:

_____
_____
_____
_____

Areas of Improvement:

_____
_____
_____

I'm grateful tonight for:

_____
_____
_____
_____

Monday

Take 5 deep breaths

> *"The most important thing in communication is hearing what isn't said."*
> *– Peter F. Drucker*

The goal written in present tense:

_____

_____

Why is this goal important:

_____

_____

_____

I'm so grateful for:

➢ _____

➢ _____

➢ _____

➢ _____

➢ _____

All In Massive Action Items

1. _____

2. _____

3. _____

4. _____

5. _____

Ideas:

_____

_____

_____

_____

Areas of Improvement:

_____

_____

_____

I'm grateful tonight for:

_____

_____

_____

Every week Actions:

Behavior/Action	Goal	M	T	W	TH	F	Sa	Su	Achieved	Net

Tuesday

Take 5 deep breaths

> *"There are four ways, and only four ways, in which we have contact with the world. We are evaluated and classified by these four contacts: what we do, how we look, what we say, and how we say it."* – Dale Carnegie

The goal written in present tense:

_____

_____

Why is this goal important:

_____

_____

_____

I'm so grateful for:

➤ _____

➤ _____

➤ _____

➤ _____

➤ _____

All In Massive Action Items

1. _____

2. _____

3. _____

4. _____

5. _____

Ideas:

_____

_____

_____

_____

Areas of Improvement:

_____

_____

_____

I'm grateful tonight for:

_____

_____

_____

_____

Wednesday

Take 5 deep breaths

> *"The time to stop talking is when the other person nods his head affirmatively, but says nothing." – Henry S Haskins*

The goal written in present tense:

_____

_____

Why is this goal important:

_____

_____

_____

I'm so grateful for:

➤ _____

➤ _____

➤ _____

➤ _____

➤ _____

All In Massive Action Items

1. _____

2. _____

3. _____

4. _____

5. _____

Ideas:

_____

_____

_____

_____

Areas of Improvement:

_____

_____

_____

I'm grateful tonight for:

_____

_____

_____

_____

Thursday

Take 5 deep breaths

> *"Doing what you love is the cornerstone of having abundance in your life." – Dr. Wayne Dyer*

The goal written in present tense:

_____

_____

Why is this goal important:

_____

_____

_____

I'm so grateful for:

➤ _____

_____

➤ _____

_____

➤ _____

_____

➤ _____

_____

➤ _____

_____

All In Massive Action Items

1. _____

_____

2. _____

_____

3. _____

_____

4. _____

_____

5. _____

_____

Ideas:

_____
_____
_____
_____

Areas of Improvement:

_____
_____
_____

I'm grateful tonight for:

_____
_____
_____
_____

Friday

Take 5 deep breaths

> *"Those who don't expect to win, don't win. It's a self-fulfilling prophecy."*
> *– Dr. Lee Pulos*

The goal written in present tense:

_____

_____

Why is this goal important:

_____

_____

_____

I'm so grateful for:

➤ _____

_____

➤ _____

_____

➤ _____

_____

➤ _____

_____

➤ _____

_____

All In Massive Action Items

1. _____

_____

2. _____

_____

3. _____

_____

4. _____

_____

5. _____

_____

Ideas:

_____

_____

_____

_____

Areas of Improvement:

_____

_____

_____

I'm grateful tonight for:

_____

_____

_____

_____

Saturday

Take 5 deep breaths

> *"It takes 20 years to build a reputation and five minutes to ruin it. If you think about that, you'll do things differently." – Warren Buffet*

The goal written in present tense:

_____

_____

Why is this goal important:

_____

_____

_____

I'm so grateful for:

➢ _____

➢ _____

➢ _____

➢ _____

➢ _____

All In Massive Action Items

1. _____

2. _____

3. _____

4. _____

5. _____

Ideas:

_____

_____

_____

_____

Areas of Improvement:

_____

_____

_____

I'm grateful tonight for:

_____

_____

_____

_____

Sunday

Take 5 deep breaths

> *"Do a little more each day than you think you can."* – *Lowell Thomas*

The goal written in present tense:

_____

_____

Why is this goal important:

_____

_____

_____

I'm so grateful for:

➢ _____

➢ _____

➢ _____

➢ _____

➢ _____

All In Massive Action Items

1. _____

2. _____

3. _____

4. _____

5. _____

Ideas:

_____

_____

_____

_____

Areas of Improvement:

_____

_____

_____

I'm grateful tonight for:

_____

_____

_____

_____

Monday

Take 5 deep breaths

> *"Nothing is permanent in this wicked world, not even our troubles."* – *Charlie Chaplin*

The goal written in present tense:

_____

_____

Why is this goal important:

_____

_____

_____

I'm so grateful for:

➢ _____

   _____

➢ _____

   _____

➢ _____

   _____

➢ _____

   _____

➢ _____

   _____

All In Massive Action Items

1. _____

2. _____

3. _____

4. _____

5. _____

Ideas:

_____
_____
_____
_____

Areas of Improvement:

_____
_____
_____

I'm grateful tonight for:

_____
_____
_____
_____

Every week Actions:

Behavior/Action	Goal	M	T	W	TH	F	Sa	Su	Achieved	Net

Tuesday

Take 5 deep breaths

> *"The only way to change your life is to make a decision and change conditions."* – Robert Pino

The goal written in present tense:

_____

_____

Why is this goal important:

_____

_____

_____

I'm so grateful for:

➤ _____

➤ _____

➤ _____

➤ _____

➤ _____

All In Massive Action Items

1. _____

2. _____

3. _____

4. _____

5. _____

Ideas:

_____

_____

_____

_____

Areas of Improvement:

_____

_____

_____

I'm grateful tonight for:

_____

_____

_____

_____

Wednesday

Take 5 deep breaths

> *"To achieve goals you've never achieved before, you need to start doing things you've never done before." – Stephen Covey*

The goal written in present tense:

_____

_____

Why is this goal important:

_____

_____

_____

I'm so grateful for:

➢ _____

_____

➢ _____

_____

➢ _____

_____

➢ _____

_____

➢ _____

_____

All In Massive Action Items

1. _____

2. _____

3. _____

4. _____

5. _____

Ideas:

_____

_____

_____

_____

Areas of Improvement:

_____

_____

_____

I'm grateful tonight for:

_____

_____

_____

_____

Thursday

Take 5 deep breaths

> *"Leave your excuses behind, and you will begin to attract wealth." – Joe Vitale*

The goal written in present tense:

_____

_____

Why is this goal important:

_____

_____

_____

I'm so grateful for:

➢ _____

_____

➢ _____

_____

➢ _____

_____

➢ _____

_____

➢ _____

_____

All In Massive Action Items

1. _____

_____

2. _____

_____

3. _____

_____

4. _____

_____

5. _____

_____

Ideas:

_____

_____

_____

_____

Areas of Improvement:

_____

_____

_____

I'm grateful tonight for:

_____

_____

_____

_____

Friday

Take 5 deep breaths

> *"Success is the sum of small efforts repeated day in and day out." –*
> *Robert Collier*

The goal written in present tense:

_____
_____

Why is this goal important:

_____
_____
_____

I'm so grateful for:

➢ _____
_____
➢ _____
_____
➢ _____
_____
➢ _____
_____
➢ _____
_____

All In Massive Action Items

1. _____
_____
2. _____
_____
3. _____
_____
4. _____
_____
5. _____
_____

Ideas:

_____

_____

_____

_____

Areas of Improvement:

_____

_____

_____

I'm grateful tonight for:

_____

_____

_____

_____

Saturday

Take 5 deep breaths

> *"Don't wish it were easier, Wish you were Better." – Jim Rohn*

The goal written in present tense:

_____

_____

Why is this goal important:

_____

_____

_____

I'm so grateful for:

➤ _____

➤ _____

➤ _____

➤ _____

➤ _____

All In Massive Action Items

1. _____

2. _____

3. _____

4. _____

5. _____

Ideas:

_____

_____

_____

_____

Areas of Improvement:

_____

_____

_____

I'm grateful tonight for:

_____

_____

_____

_____

Sunday

Take 5 deep breaths

> *"Life is inherently risky. There is only one big risk you should avoid at all costs. That is the risk of doing nothing." – Denis Waitley*

The goal written in present tense:

_____

_____

Why is this goal important:

_____

_____

_____

I'm so grateful for:

➤ _____

➤ _____

➤ _____

➤ _____

➤ _____

All In Massive Action Items

1. _____

2. _____

3. _____

4. _____

5. _____

Ideas:

_____

_____

_____

_____

Areas of Improvement:

_____

_____

_____

I'm grateful tonight for:

_____

_____

_____

_____

Monday

Take 5 deep breaths

> *"If you chase two rabbits, you will not catch either one."* – *Russian Proverb*

The goal written in present tense:

_____

_____

Why is this goal important:

_____

_____

_____

I'm so grateful for:

➤ _____

_____

➤ _____

_____

➤ _____

_____

➤ _____

_____

➤ _____

_____

All In Massive Action Items

1. _____

2. _____

3. _____

4. _____

5. _____

Ideas:

_____

_____

_____

_____

Areas of Improvement:

_____

_____

_____

I'm grateful tonight for:

_____

_____

_____

_____

Every week Actions:

Behavior/Action	Goal	M	T	W	TH	F	Sa	Su	Achieved	Net

Tuesday

Take 5 deep breaths

> *"Our minds influence the key activity of the brain, which then influences everything; perception, cognition, thoughts and feelings, personal relationships; they're all a projection of you."* – Deepak Chopra

The goal written in present tense:

_____
_____

Why is this goal important:

_____
_____
_____

I'm so grateful for:

➤ _____

➤ _____

➤ _____

➤ _____

➤ _____

All In Massive Action Items

1. _____

2. _____

3. _____

4. _____

5. _____

Ideas:

_____

_____

_____

_____

Areas of Improvement:

_____

_____

_____

I'm grateful tonight for:

_____

_____

_____

_____

Wednesday

Take 5 deep breaths

> *"It is in your moments of decision that your destiny is shaped."* –
> *Anthony Robbins*

The goal written in present tense:

_____

_____

Why is this goal important:

_____

_____

_____

I'm so grateful for:

➤ _____

➤ _____

➤ _____

➤ _____

➤ _____

All In Massive Action Items

1. _____

2. _____

3. _____

4. _____

5. _____

Ideas:

_____

_____

_____

_____

Areas of Improvement:

_____

_____

_____

I'm grateful tonight for:

_____

_____

_____

_____

Thursday

Take 5 deep breaths

"To Earn More, You Must Learn More." – Brian Tracy

The goal written in present tense:

_____
_____

Why is this goal important:

_____
_____
_____

I'm so grateful for:

➢ _____
  _____

➢ _____
  _____

➢ _____
  _____

➢ _____
  _____

➢ _____
  _____

All In Massive Action Items

1. _____
   _____

2. _____
   _____

3. _____
   _____

4. _____
   _____

5. _____
   _____

Ideas:

_____

_____

_____

_____

Areas of Improvement:

_____

_____

_____

I'm grateful tonight for:

_____

_____

_____

_____

Friday

Take 5 deep breaths

> *"Anyone who stops learning is OLD whether at twenty or eighty."* –
> *Henry Ford*

The goal written in present tense:

_____

_____

Why is this goal important:

_____

_____

_____

I'm so grateful for:

➤ _____

   _____

➤ _____

   _____

➤ _____

   _____

➤ _____

   _____

➤ _____

   _____

All In Massive Action Items

1. _____

2. _____

3. _____

4. _____

5. _____

Ideas:

_____
_____
_____
_____

Areas of Improvement:

_____
_____
_____

I'm grateful tonight for:

_____
_____
_____
_____

Saturday

Take 5 deep breaths

> *"Everyone has potential, yet almost no one is reaching it." – Noah St. John*

The goal written in present tense:

_____

_____

Why is this goal important:

_____

_____

_____

I'm so grateful for:

➤ _____

_____

➤ _____

_____

➤ _____

_____

➤ _____

_____

➤ _____

_____

All In Massive Action Items

1. _____

_____

2. _____

_____

3. _____

_____

4. _____

_____

5. _____

_____

Ideas:

_____

_____

_____

_____

Areas of Improvement:

_____

_____

_____

I'm grateful tonight for:

_____

_____

_____

_____

Sunday

Take 5 deep breaths

> *"Achievement seems to be connected with action. Successful men and women keep moving. They make mistakes but they don't quit." – Conrad Hilton*

The goal written in present tense:

_____

_____

Why is this goal important:

_____

_____

_____

I'm so grateful for:

➢ _____

➢ _____

➢ _____

➢ _____

➢ _____

All In Massive Action Items

1. _____

2. _____

3. _____

4. _____

5. _____

Ideas:

_____

_____

_____

_____

Areas of Improvement:

_____

_____

_____

I'm grateful tonight for:

_____

_____

_____

_____

Monday

Take 5 deep breaths

> *"If we do not create and control our environment, our environment creates and controls us." – Marshall Goldsmith*

The goal written in present tense:

_____

_____

Why is this goal important:

_____

_____

_____

I'm so grateful for:

➤ _____

➤ _____

➤ _____

➤ _____

➤ _____

All In Massive Action Items

1. _____

2. _____

3. _____

4. _____

5. _____

Ideas:

_____

_____

_____

_____

Areas of Improvement:

_____

_____

_____

I'm grateful tonight for:

_____

_____

_____

_____

Every week Actions:

Behavior/Action	Goal	M	T	W	TH	F	Sa	Su	Achieved	Net

Tuesday

Take 5 deep breaths

> *"When you have absolute clarity about what you want, and how you're going to get it, you're able to focus on what's important, so you get more done in less time." – Brian Tracy*

The goal written in present tense:

_____
_____

Why is this goal important:

_____
_____
_____

I'm so grateful for:

➤ _____
_____

➤ _____
_____

➤ _____
_____

➤ _____
_____

➤ _____
_____

All In Massive Action Items

1. _____
_____

2. _____
_____

3. _____
_____

4. _____
_____

5. _____
_____

Ideas:

_____

_____

_____

_____

Areas of Improvement:

_____

_____

_____

I'm grateful tonight for:

_____

_____

_____

_____

Wednesday

Take 5 deep breaths

"The key is not to prioritize what's on your schedule but to schedule your priorities." – Stephen Covey

The goal written in present tense:

_____

_____

Why is this goal important:

_____

_____

_____

I'm so grateful for:

➤ _____

_____

➤ _____

_____

➤ _____

_____

➤ _____

_____

➤ _____

_____

All In Massive Action Items

1. _____

_____

2. _____

_____

3. _____

_____

4. _____

_____

5. _____

_____

Ideas:

_____

_____

_____

_____

Areas of Improvement:

_____

_____

_____

I'm grateful tonight for:

_____

_____

_____

_____

Thursday

Take 5 deep breaths

> *"Each moment of our life, we either invoke or destroy our dreams. We call upon it to become a fact, or we cancel our previous instructions."* – *Stuart Wilde*

The goal written in present tense:

_____

_____

Why is this goal important:

_____

_____

_____

I'm so grateful for:

➢ _____

➢ _____

➢ _____

➢ _____

➢ _____

All In Massive Action Items

1. _____

2. _____

3. _____

4. _____

5. _____

Ideas:

_____

_____

_____

_____

Areas of Improvement:

_____

_____

_____

I'm grateful tonight for:

_____

_____

_____

_____

Friday

Take 5 deep breaths

> *"If you don't change, reality in the end forces that change upon you." –*
> *Stuart Wilde*

The goal written in present tense:

_____

_____

Why is this goal important:

_____

_____

_____

I'm so grateful for:

➤ _____

_____

➤ _____

_____

➤ _____

_____

➤ _____

_____

➤ _____

_____

All In Massive Action Items

1. _____

2. _____

3. _____

4. _____

5. _____

Ideas:

_____

_____

_____

_____

Areas of Improvement:

_____

_____

_____

I'm grateful tonight for:

_____

_____

_____

_____

Saturday

Take 5 deep breaths

> *"The key to growth is the introduction of higher dimensions of consciousness into our awareness." – Lao Tzu*

The goal written in present tense:

_____

_____

Why is this goal important:

_____

_____

_____

I'm so grateful for:

➤ _____

_____

➤ _____

_____

➤ _____

_____

➤ _____

_____

➤ _____

_____

All In Massive Action Items

1. _____

_____

2. _____

_____

3. _____

_____

4. _____

_____

5. _____

_____

Ideas:

_____

_____

_____

_____

Areas of Improvement:

_____

_____

_____

I'm grateful tonight for:

_____

_____

_____

_____

Sunday

Take 5 deep breaths

> *"Order and simplification are the first steps toward the mastery of a subject." – Thomas Mann*

The goal written in present tense:

_____

_____

Why is this goal important:

_____

_____

_____

I'm so grateful for:

➢ _____

➢ _____

➢ _____

➢ _____

➢ _____

All In Massive Action Items

1. _____

2. _____

3. _____

4. _____

5. _____

Ideas:

_____

_____

_____

_____

Areas of Improvement:

_____

_____

_____

I'm grateful tonight for:

_____

_____

_____

_____

Monday

Take 5 deep breaths

> *"There are few things more powerful than a life lived with passionate clarity." – Erwin McManus*

The goal written in present tense:

_____

_____

Why is this goal important:

_____

_____

_____

I'm so grateful for:

➤ _____

_____

➤ _____

_____

➤ _____

_____

➤ _____

_____

➤ _____

_____

All In Massive Action Items

1. _____

_____

2. _____

_____

3. _____

_____

4. _____

_____

5. _____

_____

Ideas:

_____

_____

_____

_____

Areas of Improvement:

_____

_____

_____

I'm grateful tonight for:

_____

_____

_____

_____

Every week Actions:

Behavior/Action	Goal	M	T	W	TH	F	Sa	Su	Achieved	Net

Tuesday

Take 5 deep breaths

> *"Successful people are simply those with successful habits." – Brian Tracy*

The goal written in present tense:

_____

_____

Why is this goal important:

_____

_____

_____

I'm so grateful for:
- ➢ _____
  _____
- ➢ _____
  _____
- ➢ _____
  _____
- ➢ _____
  _____
- ➢ _____
  _____

All In Massive Action Items
1. _____
   _____
2. _____
   _____
3. _____
   _____
4. _____
   _____
5. _____
   _____

Ideas:

_____
_____
_____
_____

Areas of Improvement:

_____
_____
_____

I'm grateful tonight for:

_____
_____
_____
_____

Wednesday

Take 5 deep breaths

> *"Anything that causes you to overreact or underreact can control you, and often does." – David Allen*

The goal written in present tense:

_____

_____

Why is this goal important:

_____

_____

_____

I'm so grateful for:

➢ _____

_____

➢ _____

_____

➢ _____

_____

➢ _____

_____

➢ _____

_____

All In Massive Action Items

1. _____

2. _____

3. _____

4. _____

5. _____

Ideas:

_____

_____

_____

_____

Areas of Improvement:

_____

_____

_____

I'm grateful tonight for:

_____

_____

_____

_____

Thursday

Take 5 deep breaths

> *"The temptation to quit and start over infects every creative process I've been in. Frustration and boredom always fuel this self-doubt." – Robert Lopez*

The goal written in present tense:

_____

_____

Why is this goal important:

_____

_____

_____

I'm so grateful for:

➤ _____

➤ _____

➤ _____

➤ _____

➤ _____

All In Massive Action Items

1. _____

2. _____

3. _____

4. _____

5. _____

Ideas:

_____

_____

_____

_____

Areas of Improvement:

_____

_____

_____

I'm grateful tonight for:

_____

_____

_____

_____

Friday

Take 5 deep breaths

> *"Transformation literally means going beyond your form." – Wayne Dyer*

The goal written in present tense:

_____

_____

Why is this goal important:

_____

_____

_____

I'm so grateful for:

➤ _____

➤ _____

➤ _____

➤ _____

➤ _____

All In Massive Action Items

1. _____

2. _____

3. _____

4. _____

5. _____

Ideas:

_____

_____

_____

_____

Areas of Improvement:

_____

_____

_____

I'm grateful tonight for:

_____

_____

_____

_____

Saturday

Take 5 deep breaths

> *"The only proper way to eliminate bad habits is to replace them with good ones." – Jerome Hines*

The goal written in present tense:

_____

_____

Why is this goal important:

_____

_____

_____

I'm so grateful for:

➢ _____

_____

➢ _____

_____

➢ _____

_____

➢ _____

_____

➢ _____

_____

All In Massive Action Items

1. _____

_____

2. _____

_____

3. _____

_____

4. _____

_____

5. _____

_____

Ideas:

_____

_____

_____

_____

Areas of Improvement:

_____

_____

_____

I'm grateful tonight for:

_____

_____

_____

_____

Sunday

Take 5 deep breaths

> *"When you can see God in small things, you'll see God in all things." –*
> *Donald L. Hicks*

The goal written in present tense:

_____

_____

Why is this goal important:

_____

_____

_____

I'm so grateful for:

➤ _____

_____

➤ _____

_____

➤ _____

_____

➤ _____

_____

➤ _____

_____

All In Massive Action Items

1. _____

2. _____

3. _____

4. _____

5. _____

Ideas:

_____

_____

_____

_____

Areas of Improvement:

_____

_____

_____

I'm grateful tonight for:

_____

_____

_____

_____

Monday

Take 5 deep breaths

> *"Our Character is basically a composite of our habits." – Stephen Covey*

The goal written in present tense:

_____
_____

Why is this goal important:

_____
_____
_____
_____

I'm so grateful for:

➤ _____
_____
➤ _____
_____
➤ _____
_____
➤ _____
_____
➤ _____
_____

All In Massive Action Items

1. _____
_____
2. _____
_____
3. _____
_____
4. _____
_____
5. _____
_____

Ideas:

_____

_____

_____

_____

Areas of Improvement:

_____

_____

_____

I'm grateful tonight for:

_____

_____

_____

_____

Every week Actions:

Behavior/Action	Goal	M	T	W	TH	F	Sa	Su	Achieved	Net

Tuesday

Take 5 deep breaths

> *"Love is misunderstood to be an emotion; actually, it is a state of awareness, a way of being in the world, a way of seeing oneself and others." – David R. Hawkins*

The goal written in present tense:

_____
_____

Why is this goal important:

_____
_____
_____

I'm so grateful for:

➤ _____
➤ _____
➤ _____
➤ _____
➤ _____

All In Massive Action Items

1. _____
2. _____
3. _____
4. _____
5. _____

Ideas:

_____

_____

_____

_____

Areas of Improvement:

_____

_____

_____

I'm grateful tonight for:

_____

_____

_____

_____

Wednesday

Take 5 deep breaths

> *"The aim of life is self-development. To realize one's nature perfectly –*
> *that is what each of us is here for." – Oscar Wilde*

The goal written in present tense:

_____

_____

Why is this goal important:

_____

_____

_____

I'm so grateful for:

➢ _____

_____

➢ _____

_____

➢ _____

_____

➢ _____

_____

➢ _____

_____

All In Massive Action Items

1. _____

_____

2. _____

_____

3. _____

_____

4. _____

_____

5. _____

_____

Ideas:

_____

_____

_____

_____

Areas of Improvement:

_____

_____

_____

I'm grateful tonight for:

_____

_____

_____

_____

Thursday

Take 5 deep breaths

> *"Believe it can be done. When you believe something can be done, really believe, your mind will find the ways to do it. Believing a solution paves the way to solution." – David J Schwartz*

The goal written in present tense:

_____

_____

Why is this goal important:

_____

_____

_____

I'm so grateful for:

➤ _____

➤ _____

➤ _____

➤ _____

➤ _____

All In Massive Action Items

1. _____

2. _____

3. _____

4. _____

5. _____

Ideas:

_____

_____

_____

_____

Areas of Improvement:

_____

_____

_____

I'm grateful tonight for:

_____

_____

_____

_____

Friday

Take 5 deep breaths

> *"To live is the rarest thing in the world. Most people exist, that is all." –*
> *Oscar Wilde*

The goal written in present tense:

_____

_____

Why is this goal important:

_____

_____

_____

I'm so grateful for:

➤ _____

_____

➤ _____

_____

➤ _____

_____

➤ _____

_____

➤ _____

_____

All In Massive Action Items

1. _____

_____

2. _____

_____

3. _____

_____

4. _____

_____

5. _____

_____

Ideas:

_____

_____

_____

_____

Areas of Improvement:

_____

_____

_____

I'm grateful tonight for:

_____

_____

_____

_____

Saturday

Take 5 deep breaths

> *"When it is obvious that the goals cannot be reached, don't adjust the goals, adjust the action steps." - Confucius*

The goal written in present tense:

_____

_____

Why is this goal important:

_____

_____

_____

I'm so grateful for:

➤ _____

_____

➤ _____

_____

➤ _____

_____

➤ _____

_____

➤ _____

_____

All In Massive Action Items

1. _____

_____

2. _____

_____

3. _____

_____

4. _____

_____

5. _____

_____

Ideas:

_____

_____

_____

_____

Areas of Improvement:

_____

_____

_____

I'm grateful tonight for:

_____

_____

_____

_____

Sunday

Take 5 deep breaths

> *"Health is a state of complete harmony of the body, mind and spirit. When one is free from physical disabilities and mental distractions, the gates of the soul open." – B.K.S. Iyenger*

The goal written in present tense:

_____
_____

Why is this goal important:

_____
_____
_____

I'm so grateful for:

➢ _____

➢ _____

➢ _____

➢ _____

➢ _____

All In Massive Action Items

1. _____

2. _____

3. _____

4. _____

5. _____

Ideas:

_____

_____

_____

_____

Areas of Improvement:

_____

_____

_____

I'm grateful tonight for:

_____

_____

_____

_____

Monday

Take 5 deep breaths

> *"My brain is only a receiver, in the universe there is a core from which we obtain knowledge, strength, inspiration. I have not penetrated into the secrets of this core, but I know that it exists." – Nikola Tesla*

The goal written in present tense:

_____

_____

Why is this goal important:

_____

_____

_____

I'm so grateful for:

➤ _____

➤ _____

➤ _____

➤ _____

➤ _____

All In Massive Action Items

1. _____

2. _____

3. _____

4. _____

5. _____

Ideas:

_____

_____

_____

_____

Areas of Improvement:

_____

_____

_____

I'm grateful tonight for:

_____

_____

_____

_____

Every week Actions:

Behavior/Action	Goal	M	T	W	TH	F	Sa	Su	Achieved	Net

Tuesday

Take 5 deep breaths

> *Business opportunities are like buses, there's always another one." –*
> *Richard Branson*

The goal written in present tense:

_____

_____

Why is this goal important:

_____

_____

_____

I'm so grateful for:

➤ _____

_____

➤ _____

_____

➤ _____

_____

➤ _____

_____

➤ _____

_____

All In Massive Action Items

1. _____

_____

2. _____

_____

3. _____

_____

4. _____

_____

5. _____

_____

Ideas:

_____

_____

_____

_____

Areas of Improvement:

_____

_____

_____

I'm grateful tonight for:

_____

_____

_____

_____

Wednesday

Take 5 deep breaths

> *"Mind is indeed the Builder... what is held in the act of mental vision becomes a reality in the material experience. We are gradually built to that image created within our own mental being."* – Edgar Cayce

The goal written in present tense:

_____

_____

Why is this goal important:

_____

_____

_____

I'm so grateful for:

➤ _____

➤ _____

➤ _____

➤ _____

➤ _____

All In Massive Action Items

1. _____

2. _____

3. _____

4. _____

5. _____

Ideas:

_____

_____

_____

_____

Areas of Improvement:

_____

_____

_____

I'm grateful tonight for:

_____

_____

_____

_____

Thursday

Take 5 deep breaths

> *"No one lights a lamp in order to hide it behind the door: the purpose of light is to create more light, to open people's eyes, to reveal the marvels around." – Paulo Coelho*

The goal written in present tense:

_____

_____

Why is this goal important:

_____

_____

_____

I'm so grateful for:

➤ _____

➤ _____

➤ _____

➤ _____

➤ _____

All In Massive Action Items

1. _____

2. _____

3. _____

4. _____

5. _____

Ideas:

_____

_____

_____

_____

Areas of Improvement:

_____

_____

_____

I'm grateful tonight for:

_____

_____

_____

_____

Friday

Take 5 deep breaths

> *"If you do what you've always done, you'll get what you've always gotten." – Tony Robbins*

The goal written in present tense:

_____

_____

Why is this goal important:

_____

_____

_____

I'm so grateful for:

➤ _____

➤ _____

➤ _____

➤ _____

➤ _____

All In Massive Action Items

1. _____

2. _____

3. _____

4. _____

5. _____

Ideas:

_____

_____

_____

_____

Areas of Improvement:

_____

_____

_____

I'm grateful tonight for:

_____

_____

_____

_____

Saturday

Take 5 deep breaths

> *"You can free yourself from aging by reinterpreting your body and by grasping the link between belief and biology." – Deepak Chopra*

The goal written in present tense:

_____

_____

Why is this goal important:

_____

_____

_____

I'm so grateful for:

➤ _____

_____

➤ _____

_____

➤ _____

_____

➤ _____

_____

➤ _____

_____

All In Massive Action Items

1. _____

_____

2. _____

_____

3. _____

_____

4. _____

_____

5. _____

_____

Ideas:

_____
_____
_____
_____

Areas of Improvement:

_____
_____
_____

I'm grateful tonight for:

_____
_____
_____
_____

Sunday

Take 5 deep breaths

> *"Whatever we plant in our subconscious mind and nourish with repetition and emotion will one day become a reality."* – Earl Nightingale

The goal written in present tense:

_____
_____

Why is this goal important:

_____
_____
_____

I'm so grateful for:

➤ _____
_____
➤ _____
_____
➤ _____
_____
➤ _____
_____
➤ _____
_____

All In Massive Action Items

1. _____
_____
2. _____
_____
3. _____
_____
4. _____
_____
5. _____
_____

Ideas:

_____
_____
_____
_____

Areas of Improvement:

_____
_____
_____

I'm grateful tonight for:

_____
_____
_____
_____

Monday

Take 5 deep breaths

> *"There are only two ways to live your life. One is as though nothing is a miracle. The other is as though everything is a miracle." – Albert Einstein*

The goal written in present tense:

_____

_____

Why is this goal important:

_____

_____

_____

I'm so grateful for:

➤ _____

_____

➤ _____

_____

➤ _____

_____

➤ _____

_____

➤ _____

_____

All In Massive Action Items

1. _____

_____

2. _____

_____

3. _____

_____

4. _____

_____

5. _____

_____

Ideas:

_____

_____

_____

_____

Areas of Improvement:

_____

_____

_____

I'm grateful tonight for:

_____

_____

_____

_____

Every week Actions:

Behavior/Action	Goal	M	T	W	TH	F	Sa	Su	Achieved	Net

Tuesday

Take 5 deep breaths

> *"What are you grateful for right now? Gratitude can shift your energy, raise your vibration, and make all your next moments even better." – Joe Vitale*

The goal written in present tense:

_____

_____

Why is this goal important:

_____

_____

_____

I'm so grateful for:

➢ _____

➢ _____

➢ _____

➢ _____

➢ _____

All In Massive Action Items

1. _____

2. _____

3. _____

4. _____

5. _____

Ideas:

_____

_____

_____

_____

Areas of Improvement:

_____

_____

_____

I'm grateful tonight for:

_____

_____

_____

_____

Wednesday

Take 5 deep breaths

> *"The key to abundance is meeting limited circumstances with unlimited thoughts." – Marianne Williamson*

The goal written in present tense:

_____

_____

Why is this goal important:

_____

_____

_____

I'm so grateful for:

➢ _____

_____

➢ _____

_____

➢ _____

_____

➢ _____

_____

➢ _____

_____

All In Massive Action Items

1. _____

_____

2. _____

_____

3. _____

_____

4. _____

_____

5. _____

_____

Ideas:

_____

_____

_____

_____

Areas of Improvement:

_____

_____

_____

I'm grateful tonight for:

_____

_____

_____

_____

Thursday

Take 5 deep breaths

> *"The most important thing about art is to work. Nothing else matters except sitting down every day and trying." – Steve Pressfield*

The goal written in present tense:

_____

_____

Why is this goal important:

_____

_____

_____

I'm so grateful for:

➢ _____

_____

➢ _____

_____

➢ _____

_____

➢ _____

_____

➢ _____

_____

All In Massive Action Items

1. _____

2. _____

3. _____

4. _____

5. _____

Ideas:

_____

_____

_____

_____

Areas of Improvement:

_____

_____

_____

I'm grateful tonight for:

_____

_____

_____

_____

Friday

Take 5 deep breaths

> *"Winning isn't everything – but wanting to win is." – Vince Lombardi*

The goal written in present tense:

_____

_____

Why is this goal important:

_____

_____

_____

I'm so grateful for:

➤ _____

_____

➤ _____

_____

➤ _____

_____

➤ _____

_____

➤ _____

_____

All In Massive Action Items

1. _____

_____

2. _____

_____

3. _____

_____

4. _____

_____

5. _____

_____

Ideas:

_____

_____

_____

_____

Areas of Improvement:

_____

_____

_____

I'm grateful tonight for:

_____

_____

_____

_____

Saturday

Take 5 deep breaths

> *"Intelligence without ambition is a bird without wings." – Salvador Dali*

The goal written in present tense:

_____

_____

Why is this goal important:

_____

_____

_____

I'm so grateful for:

➢ _____

➢ _____

➢ _____

➢ _____

➢ _____

All In Massive Action Items

1. _____

2. _____

3. _____

4. _____

5. _____

Ideas:

_____

_____

_____

_____

Areas of Improvement:

_____

_____

_____

I'm grateful tonight for:

_____

_____

_____

_____

Sunday

Take 5 deep breaths

> *"Ambition is the path to success. Persistence is the vehicle you arrive in."*
> *– Bill Bradley*

The goal written in present tense:

_____

_____

Why is this goal important:

_____

_____

_____

I'm so grateful for:

➤ _____

_____

➤ _____

_____

➤ _____

_____

➤ _____

_____

➤ _____

_____

All In Massive Action Items

1. _____

_____

2. _____

_____

3. _____

_____

4. _____

_____

5. _____

_____

Ideas:

_____
_____
_____
_____

Areas of Improvement:

_____
_____
_____

I'm grateful tonight for:

_____
_____
_____
_____

Monday

Take 5 deep breaths

> *"How am I going to live today to create the tomorrow I've committed to?" – Anthony Robbins*

The goal written in present tense:

_____

_____

Why is this goal important:

_____

_____

_____

I'm so grateful for:

- ➤ _____
- ➤ _____
_____
- ➤ _____
_____
- ➤ _____
_____
- ➤ _____
_____

All In Massive Action Items

1. _____
_____
2. _____
_____
3. _____
_____
4. _____
_____
5. _____
_____

Ideas:

_____

_____

_____

_____

Areas of Improvement:

_____

_____

_____

I'm grateful tonight for:

_____

_____

_____

_____

Every week Actions:

Behavior/Action	Goal	M	T	W	TH	F	Sa	Su	Achieved	Net

Tuesday

Take 5 deep breaths

> *"Healing is a matter of time, but it is sometimes also a matter of opportunity." - Hippocrates*

The goal written in present tense:

_____
_____

Why is this goal important:

_____
_____
_____

I'm so grateful for:

➤ _____

➤ _____

➤ _____

➤ _____

➤ _____

All In Massive Action Items

1. _____

2. _____

3. _____

4. _____

5. _____

Ideas:

_____

_____

_____

_____

Areas of Improvement:

_____

_____

_____

I'm grateful tonight for:

_____

_____

_____

_____

Wednesday

Take 5 deep breaths

> *"Make failure your teacher, not your undertaker." – Zig Ziglar*

The goal written in present tense:

_____
_____

Why is this goal important:

_____
_____
_____

I'm so grateful for:
- ➤ _____
- ➤ _____
- ➤ _____
- ➤ _____
- ➤ _____

All In Massive Action Items
1. _____
2. _____
3. _____
4. _____
5. _____

Ideas:

_____
_____
_____
_____

Areas of Improvement:

_____
_____
_____

I'm grateful tonight for:

_____
_____
_____
_____

Thursday

Take 5 deep breaths

> *"The greatest force in the human body is the natural drive of the body to heal itself – but that force is not independent of the belief system. Everything begins with belief. What we believe is the most powerful option of all." – Norman Cousins*

The goal written in present tense:

_____

_____

Why is this goal important:

_____

_____

_____

I'm so grateful for:

➤ _____

_____

➤ _____

_____

➤ _____

_____

➤ _____

_____

➤ _____

_____

All In Massive Action Items

1. _____

_____

2. _____

_____

3. _____

_____

4. _____

_____

5. _____
   _____

Ideas:

_____
_____
_____
_____

Areas of Improvement:

_____
_____
_____

I'm grateful tonight for:

_____
_____
_____
_____

Friday

Take 5 deep breaths

> *"Ability may get you to the top, but it takes character to keep you there." – John Wooden*

The goal written in present tense:

_____

_____

Why is this goal important:

_____

_____

_____

I'm so grateful for:

➢ _____

_____

➢ _____

_____

➢ _____

_____

➢ _____

_____

➢ _____

_____

All In Massive Action Items

1. _____

_____

2. _____

_____

3. _____

_____

4. _____

_____

5. _____

_____

Ideas:

_____

_____

_____

_____

Areas of Improvement:

_____

_____

_____

I'm grateful tonight for:

_____

_____

_____

_____

Saturday

Take 5 deep breaths

"You don't have to be great to start, but you have to start to be great." —
Zig Ziglar

The goal written in present tense:

_____
_____

Why is this goal important:

_____
_____
_____

I'm so grateful for:

➢ _____
_____
➢ _____
_____
➢ _____
_____
➢ _____
_____
➢ _____
_____

All In Massive Action Items

1. _____
_____
2. _____
_____
3. _____
_____
4. _____
_____
5. _____
_____

Ideas:

_____

_____

_____

_____

Areas of Improvement:

_____

_____

_____

I'm grateful tonight for:

_____

_____

_____

_____

Sunday

Take 5 deep breaths

> *"When you doubt your power, you give power to your doubt." – Leo F Buscaglia*

The goal written in present tense:

_____

_____

Why is this goal important:

_____

_____

_____

I'm so grateful for:

➤ _____

_____

➤ _____

_____

➤ _____

_____

➤ _____

_____

➤ _____

_____

All In Massive Action Items

1. _____

_____

2. _____

_____

3. _____

_____

4. _____

_____

5. _____

_____

Ideas:

_____

_____

_____

_____

Areas of Improvement:

_____

_____

_____

I'm grateful tonight for:

_____

_____

_____

_____

Monday

Take 5 deep breaths

> *"You were born to win, but to be a winner you must plan to win, prepare to win, and expect to win." – Zig Ziglar*

The goal written in present tense:

_____

_____

Why is this goal important:

_____

_____

_____

I'm so grateful for:

➤ _____

_____

➤ _____

_____

➤ _____

_____

➤ _____

_____

➤ _____

_____

All In Massive Action Items

1. _____

_____

2. _____

_____

3. _____

_____

4. _____

_____

5. _____

_____

Ideas:

_____
_____
_____
_____

Areas of Improvement:

_____
_____
_____

I'm grateful tonight for:

_____
_____
_____
_____

Every week Actions:

Behavior/Action	Goal	M	T	W	TH	F	Sa	Su	Achieved	Net

Tuesday

Take 5 deep breaths

> *"Prosperity is a way of living and thinking, and not just money or things. Poverty is a way of living and thinking, and not just a lack of money or things." – Eric Butterworth*

The goal written in present tense:

_____
_____

Why is this goal important:

_____
_____
_____

I'm so grateful for:

➤ _____
_____
➤ _____
_____
➤ _____
_____
➤ _____
_____
➤ _____
_____

All In Massive Action Items

1. _____
_____
2. _____
_____
3. _____
_____
4. _____
_____
5. _____
_____

Ideas:

_____

_____

_____

_____

Areas of Improvement:

_____

_____

_____

I'm grateful tonight for:

_____

_____

_____

_____

Wednesday

Take 5 deep breaths

> *"If you're looking for the next big thing, and you're looking where everyone else is, you're looking in the wrong place."* – Mark Cuban

The goal written in present tense:

_____

_____

Why is this goal important:

_____

_____

_____

I'm so grateful for:

➢ _____

➢ _____

➢ _____

➢ _____

➢ _____

All In Massive Action Items

1. _____

2. _____

3. _____

4. _____

5. _____

Ideas:

_____

_____

_____

_____

Areas of Improvement:

_____

_____

_____

I'm grateful tonight for:

_____

_____

_____

_____

Thursday

Take 5 deep breaths

> *"In life, lots of people know what to do, but few people actually do what they know. Knowing is not enough! You must take action."* – *Anthony Robbins*

The goal written in present tense:

_____

_____

Why is this goal important:

_____

_____

_____

I'm so grateful for:

➢ _____

➢ _____

➢ _____

➢ _____

➢ _____

All In Massive Action Items

1. _____

2. _____

3. _____

4. _____

5. _____

Ideas:

_____

_____

_____

_____

Areas of Improvement:

_____

_____

_____

I'm grateful tonight for:

_____

_____

_____

_____

Friday

Take 5 deep breaths

> *"The law of attraction is a law of nature. It is as impartial as the law of gravity." – Rhonda Byrne*

The goal written in present tense:

_____

_____

Why is this goal important:

_____

_____

_____

I'm so grateful for:

➢ _____

_____

➢ _____

_____

➢ _____

_____

➢ _____

_____

➢ _____

_____

All In Massive Action Items

1. _____

_____

2. _____

_____

3. _____

_____

4. _____

_____

5. _____

_____

Ideas:

_____

_____

_____

_____

Areas of Improvement:

_____

_____

_____

I'm grateful tonight for:

_____

_____

_____

_____

Saturday

Take 5 deep breaths

> *"Daring ideas are like chessmen moved forward. They may be beaten, but they may start a winning game."* – *Johann Wolfgang von Goethe*

The goal written in present tense:

_____

_____

Why is this goal important:

_____

_____

_____

I'm so grateful for:

➢ _____

➢ _____

➢ _____

➢ _____

➢ _____

All In Massive Action Items

1. _____

2. _____

3. _____

4. _____

5. _____

Ideas:

_____

_____

_____

_____

Areas of Improvement:

_____

_____

_____

I'm grateful tonight for:

_____

_____

_____

_____

Sunday

Take 5 deep breaths

> *"You are today where your thoughts have brought you; you will be tomorrow where your thoughts take you." – James Allen*

The goal written in present tense:

_____

_____

Why is this goal important:

_____

_____

_____

I'm so grateful for:

➤ _____

➤ _____

➤ _____

➤ _____

➤ _____

All In Massive Action Items

1. _____

2. _____

3. _____

4. _____

5. _____

Ideas:

_____

_____

_____

_____

Areas of Improvement:

_____

_____

_____

I'm grateful tonight for:

_____

_____

_____

_____

Monday

Take 5 deep breaths

> *"The only place where your dream becomes impossible is in your own thinking." – Robert H Schuller*

The goal written in present tense:

_____

_____

Why is this goal important:

_____

_____

_____

I'm so grateful for:

- ➤ _____
- ➤ _____
- ➤ _____
- ➤ _____
- ➤ _____

All In Massive Action Items

1. _____
2. _____
3. _____
4. _____
5. _____

Ideas:

_____

_____

_____

_____

Areas of Improvement:

_____

_____

_____

I'm grateful tonight for:

_____

_____

_____

_____

Every week Actions:

Behavior/Action	Goal	M	T	W	TH	F	Sa	Su	Achieved	Net

Tuesday

Take 5 deep breaths

> *"There is deep wisdom within our very flesh, if we can only come to our senses and feel it." – Elizabeth A Behnke*

The goal written in present tense:

_____

_____

Why is this goal important:

_____

_____

_____

I'm so grateful for:

➤ _____

➤ _____

➤ _____

➤ _____

➤ _____

All In Massive Action Items

1. _____

2. _____

3. _____

4. _____

5. _____

Ideas:

_____

_____

_____

_____

Areas of Improvement:

_____

_____

_____

I'm grateful tonight for:

_____

_____

_____

_____

Wednesday

Take 5 deep breaths

> *"Innovation distinguishes between a leader and a follower." – Steve Jobs*

The goal written in present tense:

_____

_____

Why is this goal important:

_____

_____

_____

I'm so grateful for:

➤ _____

➤ _____

➤ _____

➤ _____

➤ _____

All In Massive Action Items

1. _____

2. _____

3. _____

4. _____

5. _____

Ideas:

_____

_____

_____

_____

Areas of Improvement:

_____

_____

_____

I'm grateful tonight for:

_____

_____

_____

_____

Thursday

Take 5 deep breaths

"Money is only a tool. It will take you wherever you wish, but it will not replace you as the driver." – Ayn Rand

The goal written in present tense:

_____

_____

Why is this goal important:

_____

_____

_____

I'm so grateful for:

➤ _____

➤ _____

➤ _____

➤ _____

➤ _____

All In Massive Action Items

1. _____

2. _____

3. _____

4. _____

5. _____

Ideas:

_____

_____

_____

_____

Areas of Improvement:

_____

_____

_____

I'm grateful tonight for:

_____

_____

_____

_____

Friday

Take 5 deep breaths

> *"There are no constraints on the human mind, no walls around the human spirit, no barriers to our progress except those we ourselves erect." – Ronald Reagan*

The goal written in present tense:

_____
_____

Why is this goal important:

_____
_____
_____

I'm so grateful for:

- ➢ _____
- ➢ _____
- ➢ _____
- ➢ _____
- ➢ _____

All In Massive Action Items

1. _____
2. _____
3. _____
4. _____
5. _____

Ideas:

_____

_____

_____

_____

Areas of Improvement:

_____

_____

_____

I'm grateful tonight for:

_____

_____

_____

_____

Saturday

Take 5 deep breaths

> *"The human mind is our fundamental resource." – John F Kennedy*

The goal written in present tense:

_____

_____

Why is this goal important:

_____

_____

_____

I'm so grateful for:

➤ _____

➤ _____

➤ _____

➤ _____

➤ _____

All In Massive Action Items

1. _____

2. _____

3. _____

4. _____

5. _____

Ideas:

_____

_____

_____

_____

Areas of Improvement:

_____

_____

_____

I'm grateful tonight for:

_____

_____

_____

_____

Sunday

Take 5 deep breaths

> *"Healing does not mean going back to the way things were before, but rather allowing what is now to move us closer to God."* – Ram Dass

The goal written in present tense:

_____

_____

Why is this goal important:

_____

_____

_____

I'm so grateful for:

➤ _____

➤ _____

➤ _____

➤ _____

➤ _____

All In Massive Action Items

1. _____

2. _____

3. _____

4. _____

5. _____

Ideas:

_____

_____

_____

_____

Areas of Improvement:

_____

_____

_____

I'm grateful tonight for:

_____

_____

_____

_____

You've Made it! 90 days under your belt!

Now make sure you reward yourself for how far you have come! And take a short break and start doing it all over again... remember your habits will dictate your success! Let your light shine and go change the world!

Re-order your next journal and we'll see you again in 90 days.

About the Author

Kristen Judd has a very colorful background when it comes to her experience. As she really started to get serious about how to achieve her goals, she used these techniques to transform her life and career. Really investing in herself and being able to learn from some of the best have allowed her to achieve things she knew she wanted but wasn't sure of how to make it happen. THIS is how she did it!

Kristen is currently an Executive Vice President with a Financial Company and is enjoying the opportunity to change people's lives either as a client or as an agent starting their business.

Kristen currently resides in Colorado with her husband and children.

75462565R00107

Made in the USA
Columbia, SC
17 September 2019